Published by RMC Publishers
ISBN 978-1-998186-55-6

www.rmcpublishers.com

TABLE OF CONTENTS

I. INTRODUCTION

II. BREAKFAST

TABLE OF CONTENTS

III. LUNCH

TABLE OF CONTENTS

IV. DINNER

TABLE OF CONTENTS

V. SNACKS

TABLE OF CONTENTS

VI. DESSERTS

TABLE OF CONTENTS

VII. APPENDICES

IX. INDEX

Introduction

Welcome to the "Anti-Inflammatory Air Fryer Cookbook for Two," where the intersection of health and flavor converges in a culinary journey worth savoring. In the whirlwind of contemporary living, prioritizing a wellness-centric lifestyle has never been more crucial, and the choices we make on our plates play an integral role in this pursuit.

Inflammation, a natural response to injury or illness, becomes a concern when it overstays its welcome. The modern diet, laden with processed foods and an abundance of saturated fats, perpetuates the cycle of chronic inflammation.

This cookbook isn't just a compilation of recipes; it's a dedicated guide, ushering you through a delectable expedition towards inflammation reduction through the art of mindful and nutritious cooking, all effortlessly achieved within the streamlined efficiency of an air fryer.

But why anti-inflammatory, you might inquire? Beyond the immediate relief it brings to conditions like arthritis or allergies, the merits of an anti-inflammatory diet extend across a spectrum of well-being. Scientific inquiry asserts that chronic inflammation is intertwined with a myriad of health issues, from heart disease to diabetes and certain cancers. By adopting an anti-inflammatory approach to eating, we empower our bodies not only to heal and rejuvenate but to flourish, fostering longevity and overall well-being.

Now, envision combining the principles of an anti-inflammatory diet with the sheer convenience of air frying. This cookbook is meticulously crafted for the dynamic duo – those who revel in cooking for two – offering not just perfectly portioned but also healthy recipes.

These creations are not only swift and straightforward but are a celebration of flavor and healing properties. Join us on this epicurean odyssey as we unfold 75 recipes that encapsulate the joy of cooking for wellness, one crisp and nutrient-rich meal at a time.

Your journey toward a healthier, happier you commences within the pages of this cookbook, transcending mere recipes to become your unwavering culinary companion on the path to vitality.

For further reading on measurements and variations, choosing the perfect air fryer, risks and complications of chronic inflammation, a 28-day meal plan, and an index of recipes, head to the appendices at the end of the book. For now, let's get right into the recipes and start cooking!

Breakfast

Quinoa and Veggie Breakfast Bowl

Quinoa and Veggie Breakfast Bowl

2 servings

10 min

15 min

Ingredients

- 1 cup (185g) quinoa, rinsed
- 2 cups (480ml) water
- 1 cup (150g) cherry tomatoes, halved
- 1 cup (150g) bell peppers, sliced
- 1 cup (30g) spinach, chopped
- 1 zucchini, sliced (optional)
- 2 tablespoons olive oil
- 1 teaspoon turmeric powder
- Salt and pepper to taste
- Fresh herbs for garnish (optional)

Instructions

1. In a saucepan, combine quinoa and water. Bring to a boil, then reduce heat, cover, and simmer for 15 minutes or until quinoa is cooked.
2. In a mixing bowl, toss cherry tomatoes, bell peppers, and spinach with olive oil, turmeric, salt, and pepper.
3. Preheat the air fryer to 375°F (190°C).
4. Place the vegetable mixture in the air fryer basket and cook for 8-10 minutes, shaking the basket halfway through.
5. Fluff the cooked quinoa with a fork and divide it between two bowls.
6. Top the quinoa with the air-fried vegetables and garnish with fresh herbs if desired.

Notes

- Feel free to customize the veggies and seasoning according to your preferences.
- Experiment with different herbs and spices to enhance the flavor of this wholesome and nutritious breakfast bowl.

Nutritional Facts

Per Serving: **Kcal:** 400 **Fat:** 14 g **Carbs:** 60 g **Protein:** 12g **Sugar:** 4g

Sweet Potato and Chickpea Hash

Sweet Potato and Chickpea Hash

2 servings

5 min

20 min

Ingredients

- 2 medium sweet potatoes, peeled and diced
- 1 can (15 oz/425g) chickpeas, drained and rinsed
- 2 tablespoons olive oil
- 1/4 teaspoon cinnamon
- 1 teaspoon paprika
- 1/2 teaspoon garlic powder
- Salt and pepper to taste
- Fresh parsley for garnish (optional)

Instructions

1. Preheat the air fryer to 400°F (200°C).
2. In a large bowl, toss sweet potatoes and chickpeas with olive oil, cinnamon, paprika, garlic powder, salt, and pepper.
3. Place the mixture in the air fryer basket and cook for 15-20 minutes, shaking the basket occasionally.
4. Once the sweet potatoes are tender and chickpeas are crispy, remove from the air fryer.
5. Divide the hash between two plates and garnish with fresh parsley if desired.

Notes

- Ensure the sweet potatoes are diced into small, uniform pieces to ensure even cooking in the air fryer.
- Adjust seasoning according to taste preference before serving.

Nutritional Facts

Per Serving: **Kcal:** 380 **Fat:** 12 g **Carbs:** 58 g **Protein:** 9 g **Sugar:** 8g

Salmon and Avocado Toast

Salmon and Avocado Toast

2 servings

5 min

10 min

Ingredients

- 2 slices whole-grain bread
- 2 salmon filets
- 1 avocado, sliced
- 1 tablespoon olive oil
- 1 teaspoon lemon juice
- 1/2 teaspoon dill, chopped
- Salt and pepper to taste

Instructions

1. Preheat the air fryer to 375°F (190°C).
2. Rub salmon filets with olive oil, lemon juice, dill, salt, and pepper.
3. Place salmon in the air fryer basket and cook for 8-10 minutes, depending on thickness.
4. While the salmon is cooking, toast the bread slices.
5. Once the salmon is cooked, assemble by placing sliced avocado on the toast and topping with salmon.
6. Garnish with additional dill and season to taste.

Notes

- For optimal results, it's recommended to lightly oil the salmon filets before placing them in the air fryer to enhance the crispiness of the skin.
- Adjust the air frying time based on the thickness of your salmon filets and personal preference for doneness.

Nutritional Facts

Per Serving: **Kcal:** 420 **Fat:** 24 g **Carbs:** 30 g **Protein:** 24 g **Sugar:** 2g

Spinach and Feta Stuffed Mushrooms

Spinach and Feta Stuffed Mushrooms

2 servings

10 min

10 min

Ingredients

- 8 large mushrooms, stems removed
- 2 cups (60g) fresh spinach, chopped
- 1/2 cup (75g) feta cheese, crumbled
- 2 cloves garlic, minced
- 2 tablespoons olive oil
- Salt and pepper to taste
- Fresh parsley for garnish (optional)

Instructions

1. Preheat the air fryer to 375°F (190°C).
2. In a bowl, mix chopped spinach, feta cheese, minced garlic, olive oil, salt, and pepper.
3. Stuff each mushroom cap with the spinach and feta mixture.
4. Place the stuffed mushrooms in the air fryer basket and cook for 10-12 minutes until the mushrooms are tender.
5. Garnish with fresh parsley before serving.

Notes

- Ensure not to overcrowd the air fryer basket to allow proper air circulation.
- Adjust the cooking time based on the size of the mushrooms and personal preferences for doneness.

Nutritional Facts

Per Serving: **Kcal:** 180 **Fat:** 14 g **Carbs:** 10 g **Protein:** 8 g **Sugar:** 3 g

Blueberry Oat Muffins

Blueberry Oat Muffins

2 servings

5 min

20 min

Ingredients

- 1 cup (120g) oats
- 1/2 cup (60g) almond flour
- 1 teaspoon baking powder
- 1/2 teaspoon cinnamon
- 1/4 cup (60ml) maple syrup
- 1/4 cup (60ml) almond milk
- 1 egg
- 1 cup (150g) blueberries
- 1 tablespoon coconut oil, melted

Instructions

1. Preheat the air fryer to 350°F (180°C).
2. In a bowl, mix oats, almond flour, baking powder, and cinnamon.
3. In a separate bowl, whisk together maple syrup, almond milk, egg, and melted coconut oil.
4. Combine wet and dry ingredients, then fold in the blueberries.
5. Divide the batter into silicone muffin cups.
6. Place the cups in the air fryer basket and cook for 15-18 minutes until a toothpick comes out clean.

Notes

- This muffin recipe may yield 12 muffins.
- Be cautious not to overfill the muffin cups, leaving a little space at the top for the muffins to expand.

Nutritional Facts

Per Serving: **Kcal:** 120 **Fat:** 16 g **Carbs:** 38 g **Protein:** 9 g **Sugar:** 14 g

Turkey and Vegetable Egg Cups

Turkey and Vegetable Egg Cups

2 servings

5 min

15 min

Ingredients

- 4 large eggs
- 1/2 cup (75g) turkey, cooked and diced
- 1/2 cup (75g) bell peppers, diced
- 1/4 cup (10g) spinach, chopped
- 1/4 cup (30g) cherry tomatoes, diced
- 1/4 cup (30g) feta cheese, crumbled
- ¼ teaspoon turmeric
- Salt and pepper to taste
- Cooking spray

Instructions

1. In a bowl, whisk the eggs and mix in turkey, bell peppers, spinach, cherry tomatoes, turmeric, and feta cheese.
2. Grease two ramekins with cooking spray and pour the egg mixture evenly into each.
3. Place the ramekins in the air fryer basket and cook for 12-15 minutes or until the eggs are set.
4. Season with salt and pepper before serving.

Notes

- Feel free to customize the vegetable mix according to your preferences for a personalized and nutritious breakfast.
- Ensure the air fryer basket or molds are well-greased or lined with parchment paper to prevent sticking.

Nutritional Facts

Per Serving: **Kcal:** 250 **Fat:** 15 g **Carbs:** 5 g **Protein:** 20 g **Sugar:** 2 g

Veggie Omelette with Smoked Salmon

Veggie Omelette with Smoked Salmon

2 servings

5 min

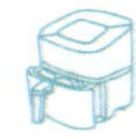
15 min

Ingredients

- 4 eggs
- 1/4 cup (30g) red bell pepper, diced
- 1/4 cup (30g) zucchini, diced
- 1/4 cup (30g) mushrooms, sliced
- 2 ounces (60g) smoked salmon, chopped
- 1 tablespoon olive oil
- Salt and pepper to taste
- Fresh dill for garnish (optional)

Instructions

1. Preheat the air fryer to 375°F (190°C).
2. In a bowl, whisk eggs and fold in red bell pepper, zucchini, mushrooms, and smoked salmon.
3. Grease a small oven-safe dish with olive oil and pour in the egg mixture.
4. Cook in the air fryer for 10-15 minutes or until the eggs are fully set.
5. Garnish with fresh dill if desired and season with salt and pepper.

Notes

- Whisk the eggs thoroughly for a fluffy omelette texture.
- Feel free to customize the vegetable fillings to your preference.

Nutritional Facts

Per Serving: **Kcal:** 320 **Fat:** 22 g **Carbs:** 5 g **Protein:** 24 g **Sugar:** 2g

Almond Flour Banana Pancakes

Almond Flour Banana Pancakes

2 servings

10 min

10 min

Ingredients

- 1 cup (96g) almond flour
- 2 ripe bananas, mashed
- 2 large eggs
- 1/2 teaspoon baking powder
- 1/2 teaspoon cinnamon
- 1/4 cup (60ml) almond milk
- 1 tablespoon coconut oil, melted
- Fresh berries for topping

Instructions

1. In a bowl, whisk together almond flour,mashed bananas, eggs, baking powder, cinnamon, almond milk, and melted coconut oil.
2. Preheat the air fryer to 350°F (180°C).
3. Grease the air fryer basket with coconut oil.
4. Pour small portions of the batter into the air fryer to make pancakes, ensuring they are well spaced.
5. Cook for 6-8 minutes, flipping halfway through, until the pancakes are golden brown.
6. Top with fresh berries before serving.

Notes

- Ensure that the pancakes are placed in a single layer in the air fryer basket, allowing for even cooking.
- Experiment with toppings such as fresh berries, a drizzle of honey, or a dollop of Greek yogurt.

Nutritional Facts

Per Serving: **Kcal:** 320 **Fat:** 22 g **Carbs:** 25 g **Protein:** 10 g **Sugar:** 10 g

Avocado Tomato Breakfast Quesadillas

Avocado Tomato Breakfast Quesadillas

2 servings

10 min

5 min

Ingredients

- 4 small whole-grain tortillas
- 1 ripe avocado, sliced
- 1 cup (150g) cherry tomatoes, sliced
- 1/2 cup (60g) feta cheese, crumbled
- 1 tablespoon olive oil
- Fresh cilantro for garnish (optional)

Instructions

1. Preheat the air fryer to 375°F (190°C).
2. Lay out the tortillas and evenly distribute avocado, tomatoes, and feta cheese on half of each tortilla.
3. Fold the other half over the filling, creating quesadillas.
4. Brush olive oil on the outside of each quesadilla.
5. Cook in the air fryer for 5-6 minutes until the tortillas are crispy and the fillings are heated through.
6. Garnish with fresh cilantro if desired before serving.

Notes

- Assemble the quesadillas just before air frying to preserve the freshness and texture of the ingredients.
- Ensure not to overfill the quesadillas to prevent ingredients from falling out during cooking.

Nutritional Facts

Per Serving: **Kcal:** 280 **Fat:** 15 g **Carbs:** 30 g **Protein:** 10 g **Sugar:** 3 g

Brussels Sprouts and Bacon Frittata

Brussels Sprouts and Bacon Frittata

2 servings

10 min

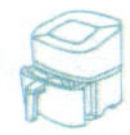
15 min

Ingredients

- 6 eggs
- 1 cup (150g) Brussels sprouts, halved
- 4 slices turkey bacon, cooked and crumbled
- 1/2 cup (60g) cherry tomatoes , halved (optional)
- 1/4 cup (30g) Parmesan cheese, grated
- Salt and pepper to taste

Instructions

1. Preheat the air fryer to 375°F (190°C).
2. In a bowl, whisk eggs and fold in Brussels sprouts, bacon, cherry tomatoes if using, Parmesan cheese, salt, and pepper.
3. Grease a small oven-safe dish with olive oil and pour in the egg mixture.
4. Cook in the air fryer for 12-15 minutes or until the frittata is set in the center.
5. Allow it to cool slightly before slicing and serving.

Notes

- Adjust cooking time as needed based on the specific model and wattage of your air fryer.
- Keep an eye on the frittata towards the end of the cooking time to prevent over-browning.

Nutritional Facts

Per Serving: **Kcal:** 330 **Fat:** 22 g **Carbs:** 8 g **Protein:** 25 g **Sugar:** 2 g

Almond Banana Stuffed French Toast

Almond Banana Stuffed French Toast

2 servings

10 min

10 min

Ingredients

- 4 slices whole-grain bread
- 2 tablespoons almond butter
- 1 banana, sliced
- 2 eggs
- 1/2 cup (120ml) almond milk
- 1/2 teaspoon vanilla extract
- 1/2 teaspoon cinnamon
- Cooking spray

Instructions

1. Spread almond butter on two slices of bread and top with banana slices. Create sandwiches with the remaining slices.
2. In a bowl, whisk together eggs, almond milk, vanilla extract, and cinnamon.
3. Preheat the air fryer to 350°F (180°C).
4. Dip each sandwich into the egg mixture, ensuring both sides are coated.
5. Place the sandwiches in the air fryer basket, ensuring they are not overcrowded.
6. Cook for 6-8 minutes, flipping halfway through, until the French toast is golden brown.
7. Serve warm and optionally dust with a bit of cinnamon.

Notes

- Ensure that the stuffed French toast is placed in a single layer in the air fryer basket to allow even cooking.

Nutritional Facts

Per Serving: **Kcal:** 380 **Fat:** 18 g **Carbs:** 40 g **Protein:** 15 g **Sugar:** 14 g

Eggs and Spinach Breakfast Burrito

Eggs and Spinach Breakfast Burrito

2 servings

13 min

7 min

Ingredients

- 2 large whole-grain tortillas
- 4 large eggs, scrambled, or fried
- 1 cup (30g) fresh spinach, chopped
- 1/2 cup (75g) cherry tomatoes, diced
- 1/4 cup (30g) shredded cheddar cheese
- 2 tablespoons salsa
- Cooking spray

Instructions

1. Preheat the air fryer to 375°F (190°C).
2. In a skillet, sauté spinach and cherry tomatoes until the spinach wilts.
3. In a separate pan, scramble the eggs.
4. Lay out the tortillas and fill each with scrambled eggs, sautéed spinach and tomatoes, shredded cheese, and salsa.
5. Fold the sides and roll into a burrito.
6. Grease the air fryer basket with cooking spray and place the burritos seam side down.
7. Cook for 5-7 minutes, turning halfway through, until the tortillas are crispy.

Notes

- Adjust the filling ingredients to your preference, such as adding black beans, avocado, or a sprinkle of your favorite herbs for extra flavor.

Nutritional Facts

Per Serving: **Kcal:** 420 **Fat:** 20 g **Carbs:** 40 g **Protein:** 20 g **Sugar:** 4 g

Eggplant and Tomato Breakfast Stacks

Eggplant and Tomato Breakfast Stacks

2 servings

10 min

10 min

Ingredients

- 1 medium eggplant, sliced into rounds
- 1 cup (150g) cherry tomatoes, sliced
- 4 eggs
- 2 tablespoons olive oil
- 1 teaspoon Italian seasoning
- Salt and pepper to taste
- Fresh basil for garnish (optional)

Instructions

1. Preheat the air fryer to 375°F (190°C).
2. Brush eggplant slices with olive oil, sprinkle with Italian seasoning, salt, and pepper.
3. Place the eggplant slices in the air fryer basket and cook for 8-10 minutes until tender and slightly crispy.
4. Meanwhile, in a pan, cook eggs to your liking.
5. Assemble by stacking eggplant rounds with sliced tomatoes and topping with a fried egg.
6. Garnish with fresh basil if desired.

Notes

- If you prefer a less chewy texture, you can lightly salt the eggplant slices and let them sit for about 15 minutes before patting them dry with a paper towel. This helps draw out excess moisture from the eggplant.

Nutritional Facts

Per Serving: **Kcal:** 280 **Fat:** 18 g **Carbs:** 15 g **Protein:** 14 g **Sugar:** 5 g

Mediterranean Egg White Frittata

Mediterranean Egg White Frittata

2 servings

5 min

15 min

Ingredients

- 4 egg whites
- 1/2 cup (75g) cherry tomatoes, halved
- 1/4 cup (30g) olives, sliced
- 1/4 cup (30g) feta cheese, crumbled
- 2 tablespoons red onion, finely chopped
- 1 tablespoon olive oil
- 1/2 teaspoon dried oregano
- Salt and pepper to taste
- Fresh parsley for garnish (optional)

Instructions

1. Preheat the air fryer to 375°F (190°C).
2. In a bowl, whisk the egg whites until frothy.
3. Add cherry tomatoes, olives, feta cheese, red onion, olive oil, dried oregano, salt, and pepper. Mix well.
4. Grease a small oven-safe dish with olive oil and pour in the egg white mixture.
5. Cook in the air fryer for 12-15 minutes or until the frittata is set.
6. Garnish with fresh parsley if desired and serve.

Notes

- Feel free to customize the Mediterranean ingredients based on your preferences.
- Adjust the cooking time if needed, as air fryer models may vary.

Nutritional Facts

Per Serving: **Kcal:** 180 **Fat:** 10 g **Carbs:** 7 g **Protein:** 15 g **Sugar:** 3 g

Apple Cinnamon Oatmeal Muffins

Apple Cinnamon Oatmeal Muffins

2 servings

7 min

18 min

Ingredients

- 1 cup (80g) rolled oats
- 1/2 cup (120ml) almond milk
- 1 large apple, grated
- 1/4 cup (60ml) maple syrup
- 1/4 cup (60ml) unsweetened applesauce
- 1 teaspoon cinnamon
- 1/2 teaspoon baking powder
- 1/4 teaspoon salt
- Cooking spray

Instructions

1. Preheat the air fryer to 350°F (180°C).
2. In a bowl, combine rolled oats, almond milk, grated apple, maple syrup, applesauce, cinnamon, baking powder, and salt.
3. Grease a muffin tin with cooking spray and fill each cup with the oatmeal mixture.
4. Place the muffin tin in the air fryer and cook for 15-18 minutes until the muffins are set.
5. Allow them to cool slightly before removing from the tin.

Notes

- This recipe makes approximately 6 standard-sized muffins.

Nutritional Facts

Per Serving: **Kcal:** 120 **Fat:** 2 g **Carbs:** 25 g **Protein:** 3 g **Sugar:** 12 g

Cauliflower and Spinach Breakfast Hash Browns

Cauliflower and Spinach Breakfast Hash Browns

2 servings

10 min

12 min

Ingredients

- 2 cups (200g) cauliflower, grated
- 1 cup (30g) fresh spinach, chopped
- 1/4 cup (30g) almond flour
- 1 egg
- 1/2 teaspoon garlic powder
- 1/2 teaspoon onion powder
- Salt and pepper to taste
- Cooking spray

Instructions

1. In a bowl, mix grated cauliflower, chopped spinach, almond flour, egg, garlic powder, onion powder, salt, and pepper.
2. Preheat the air fryer to 375°F (190°C).
3. Shape the mixture into hash brown patties.
4. Grease the air fryer basket with cooking spray and cook the hash browns for 10-12 minutes, flipping halfway through, until crispy.
5. Serve hot and enjoy.

Notes

- For optimal texture and to prevent sticking, ensure that the cauliflower and spinach mixture is well-drained before forming the hash browns. Excess moisture can affect the crispiness during air frying.

Nutritional Facts

Per Serving: **Kcal:** 150 **Fat:** 7 g **Carbs:** 15 g **Protein:** 8 g **Sugar:** 4 g

Peanut Butter Banana Wraps

Peanut Butter Banana Wraps

2 servings

6 min

7 min

Ingredients

- 2 whole-grain tortillas
- 4 tablespoons natural peanut butter
- 2 bananas, sliced
- 2 tablespoons chia seeds
- 1 tablespoon honey
- Cooking spray

Instructions

1. Lay out the tortillas and spread 2 tablespoons of peanut butter on each.
2. Arrange banana slices on top and sprinkle with chia seeds.
3. Drizzle honey over the bananas.
4. Roll up the tortillas into wraps.
5. Preheat the air fryer to 375°F (190°C).
6. Spray the wraps with cooking spray and cook for 5-7 minutes until they are crispy and golden.
7. Allow them to cool slightly before slicing.

Notes

- Lightly coat the outside of the tortilla with cooking spray or a small amount of melted coconut oil before placing it in the air fryer. This will help achieve a golden and crispy texture.

Nutritional Facts

Per Serving: **Kcal:** 380 **Fat:** 18 g **Carbs:** 50 g **Protein:** 10 g **Sugar:** 20 g

Turmeric and Coconut Breakfast Quinoa

Turmeric and Coconut Breakfast Quinoa

2 servings

10 min

10 min

Ingredients

- 1 cup (185g) quinoa, cooked
- 1/2 cup (120ml) coconut milk
- 1/2 teaspoon ground turmeric
- 1 tablespoon honey
- 1/4 cup (30g) shredded coconut
- 1/4 cup (30g) almonds, chopped
- Fresh mango slices for topping

Instructions

1. In a saucepan, combine cooked quinoa, coconut milk, ground turmeric, and honey.
2. Cook over medium heat until heated through.
3. Stir in shredded coconut and chopped almonds.
4. Preheat the air fryer to 350°F (180°C).
5. Transfer the quinoa mixture to an air fryer-safe dish and cook for 8-10 minutes until the top is slightly crispy.
6. Top with fresh mango slices before serving.

Notes

- Ensure that the quinoa is cooked and cooled before using it in the air fryer.
- Consider adding a drizzle of honey or maple syrup for a touch of sweetness if desired.

Nutritional Facts

Per Serving: **Kcal:** 380 **Fat:** 15 g **Carbs:** 50 g **Protein:** 10 g **Sugar:** 12 g

Breakfast Recipe Notes

Lunch

Grilled Lemon Herb Chicken

Grilled Lemon Herb Chicken

2 servings

5 min

25 min

Ingredients

- 2 boneless, skinless chicken breasts (400g)
- 1 lemon, juiced and zested
- 2 tablespoons olive oil
- 2 cloves garlic, minced
- 1 teaspoon dried oregano
- 1 teaspoon dried thyme
- 1 teaspoon paprika
- Salt and pepper to taste

Instructions

1. In a bowl, combine lemon juice, lemon zest, olive oil, minced garlic, oregano, thyme, paprika, salt, and pepper.
2. Place the chicken breasts in a resealable plastic bag and pour the marinade over them.
3. Seal the bag and refrigerate for at least 30 minutes.
4. Preheat the air fryer to 360°F (180°C).
5. Remove the chicken from the marinade and place it in the air fryer basket.
6. Air fry for 20-25 minutes, flipping the chicken halfway through, until it reaches an internal temperature of 165°F (74°C).
7. Let it rest for a few minutes before slicing.

Notes

- Keep an eye on the cooking time, as individual air fryers may vary slightly.

Nutritional Facts

Per Serving: **Kcal:** 300 **Fat:** 17 g **Carbs:** 2 g **Protein:** 35 g **Sugar:** 0 g

Quinoa and Roasted Vegetable Salad

Quinoa and Roasted Vegetable Salad

2 servings

5 min

15 min

Ingredients

- 1 cup quinoa (185g), rinsed
- 2 cups (300g) mixed vegetables (e.g., bell peppers, zucchini, cherry tomatoes)
- 2 tablespoons olive oil
- 1 teaspoon dried basil
- 1 teaspoon dried rosemary
- Salt and pepper to taste
- 1/4 cup (60g) feta cheese, diced

Instructions

1. Cook quinoa according to package instructions.
2. In a bowl, toss the mixed vegetables with olive oil, dried basil, dried rosemary, salt, and pepper.
3. Preheat the air fryer to 370°F (190°C).
4. Place the seasoned vegetables in the air fryer basket and cook for 12-15 minutes, shaking the basket halfway through.
5. In a serving bowl, mix the cooked quinoa, roasted vegetables, and feta.

Notes

- Ensure the air fryer basket is not overcrowded to allow even roasting of vegetables.
- Customize the salad with your favorite herbs or a squeeze of lemon for added flavor.

Nutritional Facts

Per Serving: **Kcal:** 400 **Fat:** 20 g **Carbs:** 45 g **Protein:** 12 g **Sugar:** 3 g

Salmon with Dill Sauce

Salmon with Dill Sauce

2 servings

10 min

15 min

Ingredients

- 2 salmon filets (200g each)
- 1 tablespoon olive oil
- 1 teaspoon dried dill
- 1 teaspoon garlic powder
- Salt and pepper to taste
- 2 tablespoons Greek yogurt

Instructions

1. Preheat the air fryer to 400°F (200°C).
2. Rub the salmon filets with olive oil, dried dill, garlic powder, salt, and pepper.
3. Place the salmon in the air fryer basket and cook for 12-15 minutes, depending on thickness.
4. In a small bowl, mix Greek yogurt with a pinch of dill, salt, and pepper.
5. Serve the salmon with the dill sauce on top.

Notes

- Consider marinating the salmon in the dill sauce for 30 minutes before air frying. This not only enhances the flavor but also ensures the salmon is infused with the delightful taste of dill.
- Adjust the cooking time based on the thickness of the salmon filets to ensure they are cooked to your desired level of doneness.

Nutritional Facts

Per Serving: **Kcal:** 350 **Fat:** 24 g **Carbs:** 2 g **Protein:** 30 g **Sugar:** 1 g

Sweet Potato Fries with Avocado Dip

Sweet Potato Fries with Avocado Dip

2 servings

5 min

20 min

Ingredients

- 2 medium sweet potatoes, cut into fries
- 2 tablespoons olive oil
- 1 teaspoon smoked paprika
- 1/2 teaspoon garlic powder
- Salt and pepper to taste

For Avocado Dip:

- 1 ripe avocado, mashed
- 1 tablespoon lime juice
- 1 clove garlic, minced
- Salt and pepper to taste

Instructions

1. Preheat the air fryer to 400°F (200°C).
2. In a bowl, toss sweet potato fries with olive oil, smoked paprika, garlic powder, salt, and pepper.
3. Place the sweet potato fries in the air fryer basket and cook for 15-20 minutes, shaking the basket halfway through.
4. While the fries are cooking, prepare the avocado dip by mixing mashed avocado, lime juice, minced garlic, salt, and pepper.
5. Serve the crispy sweet potato fries with the creamy avocado dip.

Notes

- Ensure that the sweet potato sticks are evenly coated with a thin layer of oil before air frying. This will help achieve a crispy exterior.

Nutritional Facts

Per Serving: **Kcal:** 280 **Fat:** 15 g **Carbs:** 35 g **Protein:** 3 g **Sugar:** 5 g

Mediterranean Stuffed Bell Peppers

Mediterranean Stuffed Bell Peppers

2 servings

5 min

20 min

Ingredients

- 2 bell peppers, halved and seeds removed
- 1 cup (185g) cooked quinoa
- 1/2 cup (75g) cherry tomatoes, halved
- 1/4 cup (40g) Kalamata olives, chopped
- 1/4 cup (30g) crumbled feta cheese
- 2 tablespoons olive oil
- 1 teaspoon dried oregano
- Salt and pepper to taste

Instructions

1. Preheat the air fryer to 375°F (190°C).
2. In a bowl, mix cooked quinoa, cherry tomatoes, Kalamata olives, feta cheese, olive oil, dried oregano, salt, and pepper.
3. Stuff the bell pepper halves with the quinoa mixture.
4. Place the stuffed peppers in the air fryer basket and cook for 15-20 minutes.
5. Garnish with extra feta and oregano before serving.

Notes

- Check for doneness by piercing the peppers with a fork – they should be tender.
- Adjust the air fryer time based on the size and thickness of the bell peppers.

Nutritional Facts

Per Serving: **Kcal:** 320 **Fat:** 18 g **Carbs:** 35 g **Protein:** 8 g **Sugar:** 6 g

Turmeric-Ginger Salmon Patties

Turmeric-Ginger Salmon Patties

2 servings

10 min

12 min

Ingredients

- 1 can (14 oz/400g) canned salmon, drained
- 1/2 cup (56g) almond flour
- 1 egg
- 1 teaspoon ground turmeric
- 1 teaspoon ground ginger
- 1/2 teaspoon garlic powder
- Salt and pepper to taste
- 2 tablespoons coconut oil (for brushing)

Instructions

1. In a bowl, combine canned salmon, almond flour, egg, turmeric, ginger, garlic powder, salt, and pepper.
2. Form the mixture into patties and place them on a plate.
3. Preheat the air fryer to 375°F (190°C).
4. Brush the salmon patties with coconut oil.
5. Air fry for 10-12 minutes, flipping the patties halfway through until they are golden brown and cooked through.

Notes

- Adjust cooking time based on your air fryer model and size, ensuring the internal temperature of the patties reaches 145°F (63°C).

Nutritional Facts

Per Serving: **Kcal:** 280 **Fat:** 18 g **Carbs:** 5 g **Protein:** 25 g **Sugar:** 1 g

Spinach and Mushroom Stuffed Chicken Breast

Spinach and Mushroom Stuffed Chicken Breast

2 servings

5 min

25 min

Ingredients

- 2 boneless, skinless chicken breasts (400g)
- 1 cup (30g) fresh spinach, chopped
- 1/2 cup (40g) mushrooms, finely chopped
- 2 tablespoons olive oil
- 1 teaspoon dried thyme
- 1 teaspoon garlic powder
- Salt and pepper to taste

Instructions

1. Preheat the air fryer to 375°F (190°C).
2. In a skillet, sauté chopped spinach and mushrooms in olive oil until they are cooked down.
3. Butterfly the chicken breasts and stuff them with the sautéed spinach and mushrooms.
4. Secure with toothpicks.
5. Season the stuffed chicken with dried thyme, garlic powder, salt, and pepper.
6. Place the stuffed chicken breasts in the air fryer basket and cook for 20-25 minutes, turning once, until the internal temperature reaches 165°F (74°C).

Notes

- Ensure that the chicken breasts are thoroughly thawed if frozen.
- The stuffing mixture can be customized with various herbs and spices to suit personal preferences.

Nutritional Facts

Per Serving: **Kcal:** 320 **Fat:** 20 g **Carbs:** 5 g **Protein:** 30 g **Sugar:** 1 g

Cauliflower and Chickpea Shawarma Bowl

Cauliflower and Chickpea Shawarma Bowl

2 servings

5 min

20 min

Ingredients

- 1 small cauliflower, cut into florets
- 1 can (15 oz/450g) chickpeas, drained and rinsed
- 2 tablespoons olive oil
- 1/2 teaspoon ground cumin
- 1 teaspoon ground coriander
- 1 teaspoon smoked paprika
- Salt and pepper to taste

For Tahini Sauce:

- 1/4 cup (60g) tahini
- 2 tablespoons lemon juice
- 1 clove garlic, minced
- Salt and pepper to taste

Instructions

1. Preheat the air fryer to 400°F (200°C).
2. In a bowl, toss cauliflower florets and chickpeas with olive oil, ground cumin, ground coriander, smoked paprika, salt, and pepper.
3. Spread the mixture in the air fryer basket and cook for 15-20 minutes, shaking the basket occasionally until cauliflower is tender and chickpeas are crispy.
4. While cooking, whisk together tahini, lemon juice, minced garlic, salt, and pepper for the sauce.
5. Serve the roasted cauliflower and chickpeas over a bed of quinoa or your preferred grain, drizzled with tahini sauce.

Notes

- For optimal results, marinate cauliflower and chickpeas in the shawarma seasoning for at least 30 minutes before air frying.

Nutritional Facts

Per Serving: **Kcal:** 380 **Fat:** 22 g **Carbs:** 35 g **Protein:** 12 g **Sugar:** 4 g

Teriyaki Turkey Meatballs

Teriyaki Turkey Meatballs

2 servings

5 min

20 min

Ingredients

- 1 pound (450g) ground turkey
- 1/4 cup (28g) almond flour
- 2 tablespoons coconut aminos (or low-sodium soy sauce)
- 1 tablespoon honey
- 1 teaspoon ginger, grated
- 1 teaspoon garlic powder
- Sesame seeds and chopped green onions for garnish

Instructions

1. Preheat the air fryer to 375°F (190°C).
2. In a bowl, combine ground turkey, almond flour, coconut aminos, honey, ginger, and garlic powder. Mix until well combined.
3. Shape the mixture into meatballs and place them in the air fryer basket.
4. Air fry for 15-18 minutes, shaking the basket halfway through, until the meatballs are cooked through and golden brown.
5. Garnish with sesame seeds and chopped green onions before serving.

Notes

- Ensure the meatballs are well-formed and not too large to ensure even cooking.
- Adjust the teriyaki sauce quantity to your taste preference.
- Serve with steamed vegetables or rice for a complete meal.

Nutritional Facts

Per Serving: **Kcal:** 280 **Fat:** 15 g **Carbs:** 8 g **Protein:** 25 g **Sugar:** 4 g

Lemon Garlic Shrimp Skewers

Lemon Garlic Shrimp Skewers

2 servings

5 min

20 min

Ingredients

- 1 pound (450g) large shrimp, peeled and deveined
- Zest and juice of 1 lemon
- 2 tablespoons olive oil
- 2 cloves garlic, minced
- 1 teaspoon dried oregano
- Salt and pepper to taste
- Wooden skewers, soaked in water

Instructions

1. In a bowl, combine shrimp, lemon zest, lemon juice, olive oil, minced garlic, dried oregano, salt, and pepper. Let it marinate for 15-20 minutes.
2. Preheat the air fryer to 375°F (190°C).
3. Thread the marinated shrimp onto the soaked wooden skewers.
4. Air fry the shrimp skewers for 6-8 minutes, turning once, until they are opaque and cooked through.

Notes

- When threading the shrimp onto the skewers, leave a small gap between each piece to allow for even cooking.
- Shrimp cook quickly, so keep a close eye on them during the air frying process.

Nutritional Facts

Per Serving: **Kcal:** 220 **Fat:** 12 g **Carbs:** 2 g **Protein:** 25 g **Sugar:** 0 g

Zucchini Noodles with Pesto

Zucchini Noodles with Pesto

2 servings

10 min

10 min

Ingredients

- 4 medium-sized zucchini, spiralized
- 1/2 cup (75g) cherry tomatoes, halved
- 2 tablespoons pine nuts
- 1/4 cup (5g) fresh basil leaves
- 2 tablespoons nutritional yeast
- 1/4 cup (60g) olive oil
- 1 clove garlic
- Salt and pepper to taste

Instructions

1. Preheat the air fryer to 375°F (190°C).
2. Toss spiralized zucchini with cherry tomatoes in a bowl.
3. In a food processor, combine pine nuts, basil, nutritional yeast, olive oil, garlic, salt, and pepper. Blend until smooth.
4. Place the zucchini and tomato mixture in the air fryer basket and cook for 8-10 minutes, tossing halfway through.
5. Drizzle the zucchini noodles with the pesto sauce before serving.

Notes

- Feel free to customize the recipe by adding grilled chicken, or any other preferred toppings for a complete and satisfying meal.
- Adjust the seasoning and pesto quantity according to personal taste preferences.

Nutritional Facts

Per Serving: **Kcal:** 250 **Fat:** 20 g **Carbs:** 10 g **Protein:** 5 g **Sugar:** 5 g

Greek Chicken Souvlaki Skewers

Greek Chicken Souvlaki Skewers

2 servings

10 min

15 min

Ingredients

- 1 pound (450) chicken breast, cut into bite-sized cubes
- 2 tablespoons olive oil
- 1 teaspoon dried oregano
- 1 teaspoon dried thyme
- 1 teaspoon garlic powder
- Juice of 1 lemon
- Salt and pepper to taste
- Wooden skewers, soaked in water

Instructions

1. In a bowl, combine chicken cubes with olive oil, dried oregano, dried thyme, garlic powder, lemon juice, salt, and pepper.
2. Let it marinate for at least 30 minutes.
3. Preheat the air fryer to 375°F (190°C).
4. Thread the marinated chicken onto the soaked wooden skewers.
5. Air fry the chicken skewers for 12-15 minutes, turning occasionally, until fully cooked and golden brown.

Notes

- Ensure that wooden skewers are soaked in water for at least 30 minutes before threading the chicken to prevent them from burning in the air fryer.
- Cut the chicken into uniform-sized pieces to ensure even cooking.

Nutritional Facts

Per Serving: **Kcal:** 280 **Fat:** 16 g **Carbs:** 2 g **Protein:** 30 g **Sugar:** 0 g

Cumin-Spiced Roasted Carrot Salad

Cumin-Spiced Roasted Carrot Salad

2 servings

5 min

20 min

Ingredients

- 4 large carrots, peeled and sliced into sticks
- 1 tablespoon olive oil
- 1 teaspoon ground cumin
- 1 teaspoon ground coriander
- 1/2 teaspoon smoked paprika
- Salt and pepper to taste
- 2 cups (90g) mixed salad greens
- 1/4 cup (30g) feta cheese, crumbled
- Chopped Walnuts (optional)

Instructions

1. Preheat the air fryer to 400°F (200°C).
2. Toss carrot sticks with olive oil, ground cumin, ground coriander, smoked paprika, salt, and pepper.
3. Spread the seasoned carrots in the air fryer basket and cook for 15-20 minutes, shaking the basket occasionally.
4. Once cooked, let the carrots cool slightly before serving on a bed of mixed salad greens.
5. Sprinkle crumbled feta cheese, and walnuts if using on top, and drizzle with additional olive oil if desired.

Notes

- Arrange the carrot slices in a single layer in the air fryer basket, allowing enough space between them. This prevents overcrowding, ensuring that each piece gets properly roasted and caramelized.

Nutritional Facts

Per Serving: **Kcal:** 220 **Fat:** 15 g **Carbs:** 20 g **Protein:** 5 g **Sugar:** 8 g

Caprese Stuffed Portobello Mushrooms

Caprese Stuffed Portobello Mushrooms

2 servings

5 min

15 min

Ingredients

- 4 large Portobello mushrooms, stems removed
- 1 cup (150g) cherry tomatoes, halved
- 1/2 cup (60g) fresh mozzarella, diced
- 2 tablespoons balsamic glaze
- 2 tablespoons fresh basil, chopped
- Salt and pepper to taste

Instructions

1. Preheat the air fryer to 375°F (190°C).
2. Place Portobello mushrooms in the air fryer basket.
3. Fill each mushroom with cherry tomatoes and mozzarella.
4. Air fry for 12-15 minutes until the mushrooms are tender and the cheese is melted.
5. Drizzle balsamic glaze over the stuffed mushrooms and sprinkle with fresh basil before serving.

Notes

- Cooking time may vary depending on the size of the mushrooms and the air fryer model. Adjust accordingly to achieve desired doneness.

Nutritional Facts

Per Serving: **Kcal:** 180 **Fat:** 12 g **Carbs:** 10 g **Protein:** 10 g **Sugar:** 5 g

Spicy Cauliflower Bites

Spicy Cauliflower Bites

2 servings

5 min

20 min

Ingredients

- 1 small head cauliflower, cut into florets
- 2 tablespoons olive oil
- 1 teaspoon smoked paprika
- 1/2 teaspoon cayenne pepper
- 1/2 teaspoon garlic powder
- Salt and pepper to taste
- 1/4 cup (60g) Greek yogurt for dipping

Instructions

1. Preheat the air fryer to 375°F (190°C).
2. Toss cauliflower florets with olive oil, smoked paprika, cayenne pepper, garlic powder, salt, and pepper.
3. Spread the seasoned cauliflower in the air fryer basket and cook for 15-20 minutes, shaking the basket occasionally.
4. Serve the spicy cauliflower bites with a side of Greek yogurt for dipping.

Notes

- Adjust the spice level by increasing or decreasing the amount of cayenne pepper according to your taste preferences.

Nutritional Facts

Per Serving: **Kcal:** 150 **Fat:** 9 g **Carbs:** 15 g **Protein:** 5 g **Sugar:** 5 g

Mediterranean Stuffed Sweet Potatoes

Mediterranean Stuffed Sweet Potatoes

2 servings

5 min

30 min

Ingredients

- 2 medium-sized sweet potatoes
- 1 cup (164g) cooked chickpeas
- 1/2 cup (164g) cherry tomatoes, chopped
- 1/4 cup (30g) olives, chopped
- 1/4 cup (30g) crumbled feta cheese
- 2 tablespoons olive oil
- 1 teaspoon dried oregano
- Salt and pepper to taste

Instructions

1. Preheat the air fryer to 400°F (200°C).
2. Pierce sweet potatoes with a fork and place them in the air fryer basket.
3. Air fry sweet potatoes for 30-35 minutes until they are tender.
4. While sweet potatoes are cooking, mix chickpeas, cherry tomatoes, Kalamata olives, feta cheese, olive oil, dried oregano, salt, and pepper in a bowl.
5. Once sweet potatoes are done, let them cool slightly, then cut them open and fluff the insides with a fork.
6. Stuff each sweet potato with the Mediterranean mixture and serve.

Nutritional Facts

Per Serving: **Kcal:** 320 **Fat:** 15 g **Carbs:** 45 g **Protein:** 8 g **Sugar:** 8 g

Garlic Parmesan Asparagus Spears

Garlic Parmesan Asparagus Spears

2 servings

10 min

10 min

Ingredients

- 1 bunch asparagus, woody ends trimmed
- 2 tablespoons olive oil
- 2 cloves garlic, minced
- 1/4 cup (25g) grated Parmesan cheese
- Salt and pepper to taste
- Lemon wedges for serving

Instructions

1. Preheat the air fryer to 400°F (200°C).
2. Toss asparagus spears with olive oil, minced garlic, salt, and pepper in a bowl.
3. Place the seasoned asparagus in the air fryer basket and cook for 8-10 minutes, shaking the basket halfway through.
4. Sprinkle grated Parmesan cheese over the asparagus during the last 2 minutes of cooking.
5. Serve with lemon wedges on the side for a zesty finish.

Notes

- Ensure your air fryer basket is well-coated with non-stick cooking spray to prevent sticking.
- Monitor the asparagus closely to achieve your desired level of crispiness.

Nutritional Facts

Per Serving: **Kcal:** 120 **Fat:** 9 g **Carbs:** 8 g **Protein:** 5 g **Sugar:** 2 g

Lemon Herb Salmon Packets

Lemon Herb Salmon Packets

2 servings

10 min

15 min

Ingredients

- 2 salmon (400g) filets
- Zest and juice of 1 lemon
- 2 tablespoons fresh dill, chopped
- 1 tablespoon olive oil
- 1 teaspoon Dijon mustard
- Salt and pepper to taste
- Sliced lemon for garnish

Instructions

1. Preheat the air fryer to 375°F (190°C).
2. In a bowl, whisk together lemon zest, lemon juice, chopped dill, olive oil, Dijon mustard, salt, and pepper.
3. Place each salmon filet on a piece of parchment paper and spoon the lemon herb mixture over the top.
4. Seal the parchment paper to create packets.
5. Air fry for 12-15 minutes until the salmon is cooked through.
6. Garnish with sliced lemon before serving.

Notes

- Ensure the packets are well-crimped along the edges to trap the steam and juices inside, enhancing the overall tenderness and taste of the salmon.

Nutritional Facts

Per Serving: **Kcal:** 300 **Fat:** 20 g **Carbs:** 2 g **Protein:** 25 g **Sugar:** 1 g

Lunch Recipe Notes

Dinner

Grilled Salmon with Sweet Potato Wedges

Grilled Salmon with Sweet Potato Wedges

2 servings

5 min

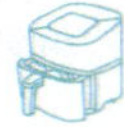
15 min

Ingredients

- 2 salmon filets (6 oz / 170 g each)
- 2 medium sweet potatoes, cut into wedges
- 2 tablespoons olive oil
- 1 teaspoon smoked paprika
- 1 teaspoon garlic powder
- 1 teaspoon dried thyme
- Salt and pepper to taste

Instructions

1. Preheat the air fryer to 400°F (200°C).
2. In a bowl, toss sweet potato wedges with olive oil, smoked paprika, garlic powder, dried thyme, salt, and pepper.
3. Place sweet potato wedges in the air fryer basket.
4. Cook for 15-20 minutes, shaking the basket halfway through.
5. Season salmon filets with salt and pepper.
6. Place them in the air fryer basket alongside sweet potatoes.
7. Cook for an additional 10-12 minutes or until salmon is cooked through.

Notes

- Choose fresh, high-quality salmon filets for the best flavor and texture. Look for wild-caught salmon if available.
- Soak the wedges in cold water for about 30 minutes before air frying to enhance their crispiness.

Nutritional Facts

Per Serving: **Kcal:** 500 **Fat:** 28 g **Carbs:** 30 g **Protein:** 35 g **Sugar:** 8 g

Mediterranean Chicken Skewers

Mediterranean Chicken Skewers

2 servings

5 min

20 min

Ingredients

- 2 boneless, skinless chicken breasts, cut into cubes
- 1 zucchini, sliced
- 1 cup (150g) cherry tomatoes
- 2 tablespoons olive oil
- 1 teaspoon dried oregano
- 1 teaspoon garlic powder
- Salt and pepper to taste
- Wooden skewers

Instructions

1. In a bowl, combine chicken cubes, zucchini slices, cherry tomatoes, olive oil, dried oregano, garlic powder, salt, and pepper.
2. Thread the chicken and veggies onto skewers.
3. Preheat the air fryer to 375°F (190°C).
4. Place the skewers in the air fryer basket.
5. Cook for 15-20 minutes, turning halfway through.

Notes

- Ensure wooden skewers are soaked in water for at least 30 minutes before threading to prevent them from burning in the air fryer.

Nutritional Facts

Per Serving: **Kcal:** 420 **Fat:** 25 g **Carbs:** 12 g **Protein:** 38 g **Sugar:** 5 g

Turmeric Chicken Thighs with Roasted Vegetables

Turmeric Chicken Thighs with Roasted Vegetables

2 servings

5 min

20 min

Ingredients

- 2 chicken thighs, bone-in and skin-on
- 1 tablespoon olive oil
- 1 teaspoon ground turmeric
- 1 teaspoon ground cumin
- 1 teaspoon paprika
- 1 teaspoon garlic powder
- 1 teaspoon onion powder
- Salt and pepper to taste
- 1 cup (71g) broccoli florets
- 1 cup (100g) cauliflower florets
- 1 cup (130g) baby carrots

Instructions

1. Preheat the air fryer to 375°F (190°C).
2. In a bowl, mix olive oil, ground turmeric, ground cumin, paprika, garlic powder, onion powder, salt, and pepper.
3. Rub the chicken thighs with the spice mixture.
4. Place the chicken thighs and vegetables in the air fryer basket.
5. Cook for 20-25 minutes or until the chicken reaches an internal temperature of 165°F (74°C).

Notes

- Ensure proper spacing in the air fryer basket to allow for even cooking of chicken thighs and vegetables.
- It's recommended to flip the chicken thighs halfway through the cooking time for a golden and crispy finish.

Nutritional Facts

Per Serving: **Kcal:** 480 **Fat:** 32 g **Carbs:** 20 g **Protein:** 30 g **Sugar:** 5 g

Spinach and Feta Stuffed Turkey Burgers

Spinach and Feta Stuffed Turkey Burgers

2 servings

5 min

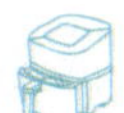

20 min

Ingredients

- 1/2 pound (225g) ground turkey
- 1 cup (30g) fresh spinach, chopped
- 1/4 cup (30g) feta cheese, crumbled
- 1 teaspoon dried oregano
- 1 teaspoon garlic powder
- Salt and pepper to taste
- Lettuce leaves for wrapping
- Tomato slices for garnish
- Avocado slices for garnish

Instructions

1. In a bowl, combine ground turkey, chopped spinach, feta cheese, dried oregano, garlic powder, salt, and pepper.
2. Form the mixture into two burger patties.
3. Preheat the air fryer to 375°F (190°C).
4. Place the turkey burgers in the air fryer basket.
5. Cook for 15-18 minutes, flipping halfway through.
6. Serve the burgers on lettuce leaves and garnish with tomato and avocado slices.

Notes

- Adjust the cooking time based on the thickness of your turkey burgers, making sure they reach an internal temperature of 165°F (74°C) to ensure they are fully cooked and safe to eat.

Nutritional Facts

Per Serving: **Kcal:** 350 **Fat:** 22 g **Carbs:** 8 g **Protein:** 30 g **Sugar:** 2 g

Balsamic Glazed Brussels Sprouts and Chicken

Balsamic Glazed Brussels Sprouts and Chicken

2 servings

5 min

25 min

Ingredients

- 2 chicken breasts, boneless and skinless
- 2 cups (300g) Brussels sprouts, halved
- 2 tablespoons balsamic vinegar
- 1 tablespoon olive oil
- 1 teaspoon honey
- 1 teaspoon dried thyme
- Salt and pepper to taste

Instructions

1. Preheat the air fryer to 375°F (190°C).
2. In a bowl, whisk together balsamic vinegar, olive oil, honey, dried thyme, salt, and pepper.
3. Toss Brussels sprouts in half of the balsamic mixture.
4. Season chicken breasts with salt and pepper, then coat with the remaining balsamic mixture.
5. Place chicken and Brussels sprouts in the air fryer basket.
6. Cook for 20-25 minutes, flipping the chicken halfway through.

Notes

- For extra flavor, marinate the chicken in a mixture of olive oil, garlic, and your favorite herbs for 30 minutes before air frying.
- Adjust the balsamic glaze and honey to your taste preferences.

Nutritional Facts

Per Serving: **Kcal:** 400 **Fat:** 20 g **Carbs:** 15 g **Protein:** 25 g **Sugar:** 6 g

Eggplant Parmesan with Tomato Sauce

Eggplant Parmesan with Tomato Sauce

2 servings

5 min

12 min

Ingredients

- 1 medium eggplant, sliced into rounds
- 1 cup (96g) almond flour
- 2 eggs, beaten
- 1 cup (240g) sugar-free tomato sauce
- 1 cup (113g) shredded mozzarella cheese
- 1/4 cup (25g) grated Parmesan cheese
- 1 teaspoon dried basil
- 1 teaspoon dried oregano
- Salt and pepper to taste

Instructions

1. Preheat the air fryer to 375°F (190°C).
2. Dip eggplant slices in beaten eggs, then coat with almond flour.
3. Place in the air fryer basket.
4. Cook eggplant slices for 10-12 minutes, flipping halfway through.
5. In a separate bowl, mix tomato sauce, dried basil, dried oregano, salt, and pepper.
6. Layer cooked eggplant with tomato sauce and cheeses.
7. Place back in the air fryer for an additional 5 minutes, until cheese is melted.

Notes

- Layering the eggplant with tomato sauce and cheese in a separate dish allows the cheese to melt evenly without making a mess in the air fryer basket.

Nutritional Facts

Per Serving: **Kcal:** 380 **Fat:** 25 g **Carbs:** 20 g **Protein:** 18 g **Sugar:** 5 g

Spicy Chickpea & Vegetable Stir-Fry

Spicy Chickpea & Vegetable Stir-Fry

2 servings

5 min

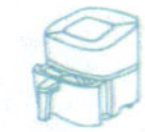
20 min

Ingredients

- 1 can (15 oz) / (425g) chickpeas, drained and rinsed
- 2 cups (150g) broccoli florets
- 1 bell pepper, sliced
- 1 cup (100g) snap peas
- 2 tablespoons soy sauce
- 1 tablespoon sriracha
- 1 tablespoon sesame oil
- 1 teaspoon ginger, minced
- 1 teaspoon garlic, minced
- Sesame seeds for garnish

Instructions

1. Preheat the air fryer to 375°F (190°C).
2. In a bowl, mix chickpeas, broccoli, bell pepper, snap peas, soy sauce, sriracha, sesame oil, ginger, and garlic.
3. Place the mixture in the air fryer basket.
4. Cook for 15-18 minutes, shaking the basket halfway through.
5. Garnish with sesame seeds before serving.

Notes

- Adjust the spice level according to your preference, and don't forget to shake the basket or stir the ingredients halfway through the cooking time for an evenly cooked and flavorful stir-fry.

Nutritional Facts

Per Serving: **Kcal:** 420 **Fat:** 15 g **Carbs:** 60 g **Protein:** 15 g **Sugar:** 10 g

Lemon Garlicky Turkey Cutlets with Asparagus

Lemon Garlicky Turkey Cutlets with Asparagus

2 servings

5 min

20 min

Ingredients

- 2 turkey cutlets
- 1 bunch asparagus, trimmed
- 2 tablespoons olive oil
- Zest and juice of 1 lemon
- 1 teaspoon garlic powder
- 1 teaspoon dried rosemary
- Salt and pepper to taste

Instructions

1. Preheat the air fryer to 375°F (190°C).
2. Rub turkey cutlets with olive oil, lemon zest, lemon juice, garlic powder, dried rosemary, salt, and pepper.
3. Place turkey cutlets and asparagus in the air fryer basket.
4. Cook for 15-18 minutes, flipping the turkey halfway through.

Notes

- When arranging the asparagus alongside the turkey cutlets in the air fryer basket, ensure they are evenly spaced to promote even cooking.
- Marinate the turkey cutlets in the lemon and garlic mixture for at least 30 minutes before air frying. This allows the flavors to infuse into the turkey, creating a more delicious and aromatic dish.

Nutritional Facts

Per Serving: **Kcal:** 350 **Fat:** 20 g **Carbs:** 10 g **Protein:** 30 g **Sugar:** 4 g

Air Fryer Cauliflower & Chickpea Curry

Air Fryer Cauliflower & Chickpea Curry

2 servings

5 min

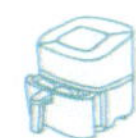
28 min

Ingredients

- 1 small cauliflower, cut into florets
- 1 can (15 oz) / (425g) chickpeas, drained and rinsed
- 1 cup (240 ml) coconut milk
- 2 tablespoons curry powder
- 1 teaspoon turmeric
- 1 teaspoon cumin
- 1 teaspoon paprika
- Salt and pepper to taste
- Fresh cilantro for garnish

Instructions

1. Preheat the air fryer to 375°F (190°C).
2. In a metal container suitable for the air fryer, add cauliflower florets and chickpeas with coconut milk, curry powder, turmeric, cumin, paprika, salt, and pepper.
3. Place the container in the air fryer
4. Cook for 20-25 minutes, shaking the basket halfway through.
5. Garnish with fresh cilantro before serving.

Notes

- Adjust the curry seasoning according to your taste preference, and feel free to add a squeeze of fresh lemon juice before serving for added freshness.

Nutritional Facts

Per Serving: **Kcal:** 420 **Fat:** 22 g **Carbs:** 45g **Protein:** 15 g **Sugar:** 8 g

Greek-style Turkey Burgers with Tzatziki

Greek-style Turkey Burgers with Tzatziki

2 servings

10 min

18 min

Ingredients

Turkey Burgers:

- 1/2 pound (225g) ground turkey
- 1/4 cup (40g) cucumber, finely diced
- 2 tablespoons red onion, finely chopped
- 1 teaspoon dried oregano
- 1 teaspoon garlic powder
- Salt and pepper to taste
- Lettuce leaves for wrapping

Tzatziki Sauce:

- 1/2 cup (120g) Greek yogurt
- 1/4 cucumber, grated and excess moisture squeezed out
- 1 clove garlic, minced
- 1 tablespoon fresh dill, chopped
- 1 tablespoon olive oil
- 1 teaspoon lemon juice
- Salt and pepper to taste

Instructions

1. In a bowl, combine ground turkey, diced cucumber, chopped red onion, dried oregano, garlic powder, salt, and pepper.
2. Form the mixture into two burger patties.
3. Preheat the air fryer to 375°F (190°C).
4. Place the turkey burgers in the air fryer basket. Cook for 15-18 minutes, flipping halfway through.
5. In a small bowl, combine Greek yogurt, grated cucumber, minced garlic, chopped dill, olive oil, lemon juice, salt, and pepper.
6. Mix well until all ingredients are incorporated.
7. Refrigerate the tzatziki sauce for at least 15 minutes before serving to allow the flavors to meld.
8. Place each turkey burger on a lettuce leaf.
9. Spoon a generous amount of tzatziki sauce over each burger.
10. Optionally, garnish with additional cucumber slices, tomatoes, or red onion.
11. Serve and enjoy!

Notes

- Serve these delightful burgers with a generous dollop of homemade tzatziki sauce for a delicious and wholesome meal.

Nutritional Facts

Per Serving: **Kcal:** 350 **Fat:** 20 g **Carbs:** 12 g **Protein:** 30 g **Sugar:** 3 g

Tofu Vegetable Stir-Fry

Tofu Vegetable Stir-Fry

2 servings

10 min

20 min

Ingredients

- 1 block firm tofu, pressed and cubed
- 1 cup (100g) broccoli florets
- 1 bell pepper, sliced
- 1 carrot, julienned
- 2 tablespoons low-sodium teriyaki sauce
- 1 tablespoon sesame oil
- 1 teaspoon ginger, minced
- 1 teaspoon garlic, minced
- Green onions for garnish

Instructions

1. Preheat the air fryer to 375°F (190°C).
2. In a bowl, toss tofu, broccoli, bell pepper, carrot, teriyaki sauce, sesame oil, ginger, and garlic.
3. Place the mixture in the air fryer basket.
4. Cook for 15-18 minutes, shaking the basket halfway through.
5. Garnish with chopped green onions before serving.

Notes

- Make sure to press the tofu before marinating to remove excess water. This can be done by placing the tofu between paper towels and applying gentle pressure for 15-30 minutes.

Nutritional Facts

Per Serving: **Kcal:** 320 **Fat:** 18 g **Carbs:** 25 g **Protein:** 18 g **Sugar:** 8 g

Air Fried Cilantro Lime Shrimp with Avocado Salsa

Air Fried Cilantro Lime Shrimp with Avocado Salsa

2 servings

10 min

10 min

Ingredients

- 12 large shrimp, peeled and deveined
- Zest and juice of 1 lime
- 2 tablespoons fresh cilantro, chopped
- 1 tablespoon olive oil
- 1 avocado, diced
- 1/2 cup (75g) cherry tomatoes, halved
- Salt and pepper to taste

Instructions

1. Preheat the air fryer to 375°F (190°C).
2. In a bowl, toss shrimp with lime zest, lime juice, chopped cilantro, olive oil, salt, and pepper.
3. Place shrimp in the air fryer basket.
4. Air Fry for 8-10 minutes.
5. In another bowl, combine diced avocado and cherry tomatoes to make salsa.
6. Serve shrimp over the salsa.

Notes

- Marinate the shrimp for 15-30 minutes before air frying to allow the flavors to infuse into the shrimp.

Nutritional Facts

Per Serving: **Kcal:** 280 **Fat:** 18 g **Carbs:** 15 g **Protein:** 20 g **Sugar:** 3 g

Pesto Chicken with Roasted Veggies

Pesto Chicken with Roasted Veggies

2 servings

5 min

25 min

Ingredients

- 2 chicken breasts, boneless and skinless
- 1 cup (240g) cherry tomatoes
- 1 cup (150g) baby potatoes, halved
- 2 tablespoons pesto sauce
- 1 tablespoon olive oil
- 1 teaspoon dried basil
- Salt and pepper to taste

Instructions

1. Preheat the air fryer to 375°F (190°C).
2. Rub chicken breasts with pesto sauce, olive oil, dried basil, salt, and pepper.
3. Place chicken, cherry tomatoes, and baby potatoes in the air fryer basket.
4. Air Fry for 20-25 minutes, flipping the chicken halfway through.

Notes

- When arranging vegetables in the air fryer basket, spread them out evenly to avoid overcrowding. This promotes better air circulation and ensures that each vegetable gets roasted to perfection.

Nutritional Facts

Per Serving: **Kcal:** 420 **Fat:** 20 g **Carbs:** 30 g **Protein:** 30 g **Sugar:** 4 g

Butternut Squash and Chickpea Buddha Bowl

Butternut Squash and Chickpea Buddha Bowl

2 servings

5 min

20 min

Ingredients

- 2 cups (400g) butternut squash, cubed
- 1 can (15 oz) / (425g) chickpeas, drained and rinsed
- 1 tablespoon olive oil
- 1/2 teaspoon cumin
- 1 teaspoon smoked paprika
- Salt and pepper to taste
- 2 cups (130g) kale, chopped
- 1/4 cup (60g) tahini
- 1 tablespoon lemon juice

Instructions

1. Preheat the air fryer to 375°F (190°C).
2. Toss butternut squash and chickpeas with olive oil, cumin, smoked paprika, salt, and pepper.
3. Place the mixture in the air fryer basket.
4. Cook for 20-25 minutes, shaking the basket halfway through.
5. In a bowl, massage kale with tahini and lemon juice.
6. Serve the roasted butternut squash and chickpeas over the kale.

Notes

- Feel free to customize the bowl with additional toppings such as avocado, cherry tomatoes, or a sprinkle of your favorite herbs.

Nutritional Facts

Per Serving: **Kcal:** 380 **Fat:** 18 g **Carbs:** 45 g **Protein:** 15 g **Sugar:** 8 g

Caprese Stuffed Chicken Breasts

Caprese Stuffed Chicken Breasts

2 servings

5 min

22 min

Ingredients

- 2 chicken breasts, boneless and skinless
- 1/2 cup (75g) cherry tomatoes, halved
- 1/4 cup (28g) fresh mozzarella cheese, diced
- 2 tablespoons balsamic glaze
- 1 tablespoon olive oil
- 1 teaspoon dried basil
- Salt and pepper to taste

Instructions

1. Preheat the air fryer to 375°F (190°C).
2. Cut a pocket into each chicken breast.
3. Stuff each chicken breast with cherry tomatoes and mozzarella.
4. Rub chicken with olive oil, dried basil, salt, and pepper.
5. Place the stuffed chicken breasts in the air fryer basket.
6. Air Fry for 18-22 minutes.

Notes

- Make sure to use toothpicks to secure the openings of the stuffed chicken breasts.

Nutritional Facts

Per Serving: **Kcal:** 340 **Fat:** 20 g **Carbs:** 10 g **Protein:** 30 g **Sugar:** 5 g

Moroccan Style Spiced Chicken Thighs with Cauliflower Rice

Moroccan Style Spiced Chicken Thighs with Cauliflower Rice

2 servings

5 min

20 min

Ingredients

- 2 chicken thighs, bone-in and skin-on
- 1 head cauliflower, grated (for cauliflower rice)
- 2 tablespoons olive oil
- 1/2 teaspoon ground cumin
- 1 teaspoon ground coriander
- 1 teaspoon smoked paprika
- 1 teaspoon cinnamon
- Salt and pepper to taste
- Fresh parsley for garnish

Instructions

1. Preheat the air fryer to 375°F (190°C).
2. Rub chicken thighs with olive oil, ground cumin, ground coriander, smoked paprika, cinnamon, salt, and pepper.
3. Place chicken thighs in the air fryer basket.
4. Cook for 20-25 minutes, flipping halfway through.
5. Meanwhile, in a pan, sauté grated cauliflower with a bit of olive oil over medium heat until tender.
6. Serve the chicken thighs over cauliflower rice and garnish with fresh parsley.

Notes

- Make sure to generously coat the chicken thighs with the spice mix, allowing them to marinate for at least 30 minutes.

Nutritional Facts

Per Serving: **Kcal:** 420 **Fat:** 25 g **Carbs:** 15 g **Protein:** 30 g **Sugar:** 5 g

Lemon Herb Cod with Roasted Broccoli

Lemon Herb Cod with Roasted Broccoli

2 servings

5 min

15 min

Ingredients

- 2 cod filets
- 1 bunch broccoli, cut into florets
- Zest and juice of 1 lemon
- 2 tablespoons olive oil
- 1 teaspoon dried thyme
- 1 teaspoon dried dill
- Salt and pepper to taste

Instructions

1. Preheat the air fryer to 375°F (190°C).
2. Rub cod filets with olive oil, lemon zest, lemon juice, dried thyme, dried dill, salt, and pepper.
3. Place cod filets and broccoli florets in the air fryer basket.
4. Cook for 10-15 minutes, flipping the cod halfway through.

Notes

- Adjust cooking times based on the thickness of the cod filets to achieve a perfectly flaky and moist texture.
- For a crisper texture, pat the cod filets dry with a paper towel before applying the marinade.

Nutritional Facts

Per Serving: **Kcal:** 320 **Fat:** 18 g **Carbs:** 10 g **Protein:** 30 g **Sugar:** 4 g

Spaghetti Squash with Pesto Grilled Shrimp

Spaghetti Squash with Pesto Grilled Shrimp

2 servings

5 min

25 min

Ingredients

- 1 medium spaghetti squash, halved and seeds removed
- 12 large shrimp, peeled and deveined
- 2 tablespoons pesto sauce
- 1 tablespoon olive oil
- 1 teaspoon dried basil
- Salt and pepper to taste
- Fresh parsley for garnish

Instructions

1. Preheat the air fryer to 375°F (190°C).
2. Rub spaghetti squash with olive oil, dried basil, salt, and pepper.
3. Place the spaghetti squash in the air fryer basket. Air Fry for 20-25 minutes. Set aside to cool.
4. In a bowl, toss shrimp with pesto sauce.
5. Place the pesto-coated shrimp in the air fryer basket. Cook for an additional 5-7 minutes.
6. Scrape the spaghetti squash with a fork to create "noodles" and top with grilled shrimp.
7. Garnish with fresh parsley before serving.

Notes

- For the best results with your spaghetti squash, pierce it with a fork a few times before air frying. This will allow steam to escape during cooking and prevent the squash from bursting.

Nutritional Facts

Per Serving: **Kcal:** 320 **Fat:** 18 g **Carbs:** 20 g **Protein:** 25 g **Sugar:** 5 g

Dinner Recipe Notes

Snacks

Sweet Potato Chips

Sweet Potato Chips

2 servings

10 min

15 min

Ingredients

- 2 medium sweet potatoes, thinly sliced
- 1 tablespoon olive oil
- 1 teaspoon turmeric
- 1 teaspoon paprika
- 1/2 teaspoon sea salt

Instructions

1. Preheat the Air Fryer to 375°F (190°C).
2. In a bowl, toss sweet potato slices with olive oil, turmeric, paprika, and sea salt.
3. Arrange slices in a single layer in the Air Fryer basket.
4. Cook for 12-15 minutes, shaking the basket halfway through.
5. Once crispy, remove and let cool for a few minutes before serving.

Notes

- Pat the sweet potato slices completely dry with a paper towel before tossing them with oil and seasonings. Excess moisture can hinder crispiness.
- Arrange the sweet potato slices in a single layer in the air fryer basket, ensuring they don't overlap. This allows for even cooking and crispiness on all sides.

Nutritional Facts

Per Serving: **Kcal:** 120 **Fat:** 2 g **Carbs:** 25 g **Protein:** 2 g **Sugar:** 5 g

Garlic Parmesan Zucchini Chips

Garlic Parmesan Zucchini Chips

2 servings

5 min

10 min

Ingredients

- 2 medium zucchinis, thinly sliced
- 1 tablespoon olive oil
- 2 cloves garlic, minced
- 2 tablespoons grated Parmesan cheese
- 1/2 teaspoon black pepper

Instructions

1. Preheat the Air Fryer to 400°F (200°C).
2. Toss zucchini slices with olive oil, minced garlic, Parmesan, and black pepper.
3. Arrange slices in a single layer in the Air Fryer basket.
4. Air Fry for 8-10 minutes, flipping halfway through.
5. Sprinkle with additional parmesan before serving.

Notes

- Keep an eye on the chips towards the end of the cooking time to prevent over-browning.
- Feel free to customize the seasoning to your liking or sprinkle extra Parmesan for an enhanced taste.

Nutritional Facts

Per Serving: **Kcal:** 90 **Fat:** 5 g **Carbs:** 8 g **Protein:** 5 g **Sugar:** 3 g

Turmeric Roasted Chickpeas

Turmeric Roasted Chickpeas

2 servings

5 min

20 min

Ingredients

- 1 can (15 oz) / (425g) chickpeas, drained and rinsed
- 1 tablespoon olive oil
- 1 teaspoon ground turmeric
- 1/2 teaspoon cumin
- 1/2 teaspoon smoked paprika
- 1/2 teaspoon sea salt

Instructions

1. Preheat the Air Fryer to 400°F (200°C).
2. In a bowl, toss chickpeas with olive oil, turmeric, cumin, smoked paprika, and sea salt.
3. Spread chickpeas in the Air Fryer basket in a single layer.
4. Cook for 15-18 minutes, shaking the basket halfway through.

Notes

- Feel free to customize the seasoning according to your taste preferences, and adjust the cooking time based on your air fryer model to achieve the desired crunchiness.

Nutritional Facts

Per Serving: **Kcal:** 150 **Fat:** 4 g **Carbs:** 23 g **Protein:** 7 g **Sugar:** 4 g

Kale Chips

Kale Chips

2 servings

7 min

7 min

Ingredients

- 4 cups (260g) kale, stems removed and torn into bite-sized pieces
- 1 tablespoon olive oil
- 1/2 teaspoon garlic powder
- 1/2 teaspoon onion powder
- 1/4 teaspoon chili powder
- Salt to taste

Instructions

1. Preheat the Air Fryer to 350°F (180°C).
2. Massage kale with olive oil, garlic powder, onion powder, chili powder, and salt in a large bowl.
3. Spread kale in a single layer in the Air Fryer basket.
4. Cook for 5-7 minutes, shaking the basket halfway through.

Notes

- It's crucial to monitor the cooking process closely to prevent burning, as air fryer temperatures may vary.
- Experiment with seasoning options to find your preferred flavor profile.

Nutritional Facts

Per Serving: **Kcal:** 60 **Fat:** 2 g **Carbs:** 8 g **Protein:** 3 g **Sugar:** 1 g

Air Fried Salmon Bites

Air Fried Salmon Bites

2 servings

5 min

10 min

Ingredients

- 1/2 lb (225g) salmon filet, cut into bite-sized cubes
- 1 tablespoon olive oil
- 1 teaspoon turmeric
- 1/2 teaspoon cayenne pepper
- Salt and pepper to taste

Instructions

1. Preheat the Air Fryer to 400°F (200°C).
2. Toss salmon cubes with olive oil, turmeric, cayenne pepper, salt, and pepper.
3. Arrange salmon in a single layer in the Air Fryer basket.
4. Cook for 6-8 minutes until salmon is cooked through.

Notes

- For optimal results, choose fresh and high-quality salmon filets for this recipe.
- Serve these salmon bites with a side of fresh lemon wedges and your favorite dipping sauce for a delicious and healthy seafood snack!

Nutritional Facts

Per Serving: **Kcal:** 180 **Fat:** 11 g **Carbs:** 0 g **Protein:** 20 g **Sugar:** 0 g

Crispy Brussels Sprouts

Crispy Brussels Sprouts

2 servings

5 min

12 min

Ingredients

- 2 cups (300g) Brussels sprouts, halved
- 1 tablespoon olive oil
- 1 teaspoon balsamic vinegar
- 1/2 teaspoon garlic powder
- Salt and pepper to taste

Instructions

1. Preheat the Air Fryer to 375°F (190°C).
2. Toss Brussels sprouts with olive oil, balsamic vinegar, garlic powder, salt, and pepper.
3. Arrange Brussels sprouts in a single layer in the Air Fryer basket.
4. Cook for 10-12 minutes, shaking the basket halfway through.

Notes

- Achieve the perfect crispiness by ensuring the Brussels sprouts are well-dried before air frying. After washing and trimming, pat them thoroughly with a paper towel to remove excess moisture.

Nutritional Facts

Per Serving: **Kcal:** 70 **Fat:** 3 g **Carbs:** 10 g **Protein:** 3 g **Sugar:** 3 g

Sesame Ginger Edamame

Sesame Ginger Edamame

2 servings

5 min

10 min

Ingredients

- 2 cups (300g) edamame (fresh or thawed if frozen)
- 1 tablespoon soy sauce
- 1 teaspoon sesame oil
- 1/2 teaspoon grated ginger
- 1 tablespoon sesame seeds

Instructions

1. Preheat the Air Fryer to 375°F (190°C).
2. In a bowl, toss edamame with soy sauce, sesame oil, ginger, and sesame seeds.
3. Spread edamame in a single layer in the Air Fryer basket.
4. Cook for 8-10 minutes, shaking the basket halfway through.

Notes

- Shake the basket during cooking to ensure even crispiness.
- Adjust soy sauce and sesame oil according to personal taste preferences.

Nutritional Facts

Per Serving: **Kcal:** 120 **Fat:** 5 g **Carbs:** 8 g **Protein:** 10 g **Sugar:** 2 g

Coconut Crusted Shrimp

Coconut Crusted Shrimp

2 servings

5 min

10 min

Ingredients

- 1/2 lb (225g) large shrimp, peeled and deveined
- 2 tablespoons shredded coconut
- 1 tablespoon coconut flour
- 1/2 teaspoon turmeric
- 1/4 teaspoon garlic powder
- Salt and pepper to taste

Instructions

1. Preheat the Air Fryer to 375°F (190°C).
2. In a bowl, combine shredded coconut, coconut flour, turmeric, garlic powder, salt, and pepper.
3. Coat each shrimp in the coconut mixture and place in the Air Fryer basket.
4. Cook for 8-10 minutes until shrimp are golden and crispy.

Notes

- Lightly spray or brush the air fryer basket with coconut oil to prevent sticking and achieve a golden-brown crust.
- Keep a close eye on the shrimp towards the end of the cooking time to avoid overcooking, as air fryer models may vary.

Nutritional Facts

Per Serving: **Kcal:** 160 **Fat:** 7 g **Carbs:** 5 g **Protein:** 20 g **Sugar:** 1 g

Cinnamon Apple Chips

Cinnamon Apple Chips

2 servings

5 min

10 min

Ingredients

- 2 apples, thinly sliced
- 1 tablespoon coconut oil, melted
- 1 teaspoon ground cinnamon
- 1/2 teaspoon nutmeg
- 1 tablespoon maple syrup (optional)

Instructions

1. Preheat the Air Fryer to 350°F (180°C).
2. In a bowl, toss apple slices with melted coconut oil, cinnamon, nutmeg, and maple syrup (if using).
3. Arrange slices in a single layer in the Air Fryer basket.
4. Cook for 8-10 minutes, flipping halfway through.
5. Allow the chips to cool before serving.

Notes

- Keep an eye on the apple slices towards the end of the cooking time to prevent burning.
- The thickness of the slices may affect the cooking time, so adjust as needed.

Nutritional Facts

Per Serving: **Kcal:** 80 **Fat:** 1 g **Carbs:** 20 g **Protein:** 0.5 g **Sugar:** 14 g

Coconut Curry Chickpea Poppers

Coconut Curry Chickpea Poppers

2 servings

5 min

20 min

Ingredients

- 1 can (15 oz) / (425g) chickpeas, drained and rinsed
- 1 tablespoon coconut oil, melted
- 1 teaspoon curry powder
- 1/2 teaspoon turmeric
- 1/4 teaspoon cayenne pepper
- Salt, to taste

Instructions

1. Preheat the Air Fryer to 400°F (200°C).
2. In a bowl, toss chickpeas with melted coconut oil, curry powder, turmeric, cayenne pepper, and salt.
3. Spread chickpeas in a single layer in the Air Fryer basket.
4. Cook for 15-18 minutes, shaking the basket halfway through.

Notes

- Ensure chickpeas are thoroughly drained and pat-dried before tossing with the coconut curry seasoning. This will help achieve a crispy texture during air frying.

Nutritional Facts

Per Serving: **Kcal:** 160 **Fat:** 6 g **Carbs:** 22 g **Protein:** 6 g **Sugar:** 3 g

Sweet and Spicy Roasted Nuts

Sweet and Spicy Roasted Nuts

2 servings

5 min

10 min

Ingredients

- 1 cup (150g) mixed nuts (almonds, walnuts, cashews)
- 1 tablespoon maple syrup
- 1/2 teaspoon ground cinnamon
- 1/4 teaspoon cayenne pepper
- 1/4 teaspoon sea salt

Instructions

1. Preheat the Air Fryer to 350°F (180°C).
2. In a bowl, toss mixed nuts with maple syrup, ground cinnamon, cayenne pepper, and sea salt.
3. Spread the nuts in a single layer in the Air Fryer basket.
4. Cook for 8-10 minutes, shaking the basket halfway through.
5. Allow the nuts to cool before serving.

Notes

- For optimal results, ensure to spread the nuts evenly in the air fryer basket, allowing for proper air circulation.
- Once done, allow the nuts to cool completely before serving to enhance their crunchiness.

Nutritional Facts

Per Serving: **Kcal:** 180 **Fat:** 14 g **Carbs:** 9g **Protein:** 5 g **Sugar:** 3 g

Snack Recipe Notes

Desserts

Turmeric Banana Bites

Turmeric Banana Bites

2 servings

5 min

7 min

Ingredients

- 2 bananas, sliced
- 1 tablespoon coconut oil
- 1 teaspoon ground turmeric
- 1 tablespoon chopped walnuts

Instructions

1. Preheat the air fryer to 350°F (175°C).
2. Toss banana slices in melted coconut oil and turmeric.
3. Place banana slices in the air fryer and cook for 5-7 minutes.
4. Sprinkle with chopped walnuts before serving.

Notes

- Make sure to keep an eye on the bananas during the air frying process to prevent overcooking.
- The turmeric not only adds a unique flavor but also provides anti-inflammatory benefits.

Nutritional Facts

Per Serving: **Kcal:** 140 **Fat:** 7 g **Carbs:** 20 g **Protein:** 2 g **Sugar:** 12 g

Gingered Peach Slices

Gingered Peach Slices

2 servings

5 min

8 min

Ingredients

- 2 peaches, sliced
- 1 tablespoon melted coconut oil
- 1 teaspoon ground ginger
- 1 tablespoon chopped mint (optional)

Instructions

1. Preheat the air fryer to 360°F (180°C).
2. Toss peach slices in melted coconut oil and ground ginger.
3. Air fry for 6-8 minutes until peaches are tender.
4. Garnish with chopped mint before serving.

Notes

- Choose ripe peaches for a sweeter and juicier flavor. The natural sugars in ripe peaches caramelize beautifully during the air frying process.
- Ensure the peach slices are of uniform thickness to promote even cooking. This helps achieve a perfect balance between a soft, tender inside and a slightly caramelized exterior.

Nutritional Facts

Per Serving: **Kcal:** 100 **Fat:** 2 g **Carbs:** 25 g **Protein:** 1 g **Sugar:** 18 g

Air Fryer Pumpkin Spice Apples

Air Fryer Pumpkin Spice Apples

2 servings

5 min

12 min

Ingredients

- 2 apples, cored and halved
- 2 tablespoons pumpkin puree
- 1 teaspoon cinnamon
- 1 tablespoon chopped pecans, or walnuts
- 1 tablespoon maple syrup

Instructions

1. Preheat the air fryer to 360°F (180°C).
2. In a bowl, mix pumpkin puree, cinnamon, chopped pecans, and maple syrup.
3. Fill each apple half with the mixture.
4. Air fry for 10-12 minutes until apples are tender.

Notes

- Choose firm apples like Honeycrisp or Granny Smith for a satisfying crunch after air frying.
- Lightly spray or brush the apple halves with oil before air frying to promote crispiness and prevent sticking.

Nutritional Facts

Per Serving: **Kcal:** 180 **Fat:** 5 g **Carbs:** 35 g **Protein:** 2 g **Sugar:** 25 g

Mint Chocolate Zucchini Bites

Mint Chocolate Zucchini Bites

2 servings

5 min

10 min

Ingredients

- 1 cup (120g) shredded zucchini
- 1/4 cup (25g) cocoa powder
- 1/4 cup (28g) almond flour
- 2 tablespoons honey
- 1/2 teaspoon peppermint extract

Instructions

1. Preheat the air fryer to 350°F (175°C).
2. In a bowl, combine shredded zucchini, cocoa powder, almond flour, honey, and peppermint extract.
3. Form small bites and place them in the air fryer basket.
4. Air fry for 8-10 minutes until firm.

Notes

- When air frying, monitor the cooking time closely to prevent overcooking, as air fryer temperatures may vary.
- Adjust the sweetness by varying the amount of honey based on your preference.

Nutritional Facts

Per Serving: **Kcal:** 120 **Fat:** 4 g **Carbs:** 20 g **Protein:** 3 g **Sugar:** 12 g

Air Fryer Blueberry Oat Crisp

Air Fryer Blueberry Oat Crisp

2 servings

5 min

15 min

Ingredients

- 1 cup (148g) blueberries
- 1/2 cup (40g) rolled oats
- 2 tablespoons almond flour
- 1 tablespoon coconut oil
- 1 tablespoon honey

Instructions

1. In a bowl, mix blueberries with rolled oats, almond flour, melted coconut oil, and honey.
2. Transfer to an air fryer-safe dish.
3. Air fry at 350°F (175°C) for 12-15 minutes until the top is crisp.

Notes

- Cooking times may vary slightly based on different air fryer models, so adjust as needed to achieve the desired level of crispiness.

Nutritional Facts

Per Serving: **Kcal:** 180 **Fat:** 6 g **Carbs:** 30 g **Protein:** 3 g **Sugar:** 15 g

Lemon Blueberry Almond Cake

Lemon Blueberry Almond Cake

2 servings

5 min

18 min

Ingredients

- 1/2 cup (50g) almond flour
- 2 tablespoons coconut flour
- 1/2 teaspoon baking powder
- 2 tablespoons almond butter
- 2 tablespoons honey
- Zest and juice of 1 lemon
- 1/4 cup (35g) blueberries

Instructions

1. Preheat the air fryer to 350°F (175°C).
2. In a bowl, mix almond flour, coconut flour, baking powder, almond butter, honey, lemon zest, and lemon juice.
3. Fold in blueberries.
4. Pour the batter into a greased air fryer-safe dish.
5. Air fry for 15-18 minutes until a toothpick comes out clean from the center.

Notes

- Serve the cake with a dollop of Greek yogurt or a scoop of vanilla ice cream for a creamy contrast.
- A drizzle of honey or a sprinkle of sliced almonds on top can add both sweetness and crunch.

Nutritional Facts

Per Serving: **Kcal:** 200 **Fat:** 12 g **Carbs:** 20 g **Protein:** 5 g **Sugar:** 10 g

Orange Ginger Carrot Cake Bites

Orange Ginger Carrot Cake Bites

2 servings

5 min

12 min

Ingredients

- 1 cup (110g) shredded carrots
- 1/4 cup (28g) almond flour
- 1/4 cup (20g) shredded coconut
- 2 tablespoons raisins
- 1 teaspoon ground ginger
- Zest of 1 orange

Instructions

1. In a bowl, combine shredded carrots, almond flour, shredded coconut, raisins, ground ginger, and orange zest.
2. Form small bites and place them in the air fryer basket.
3. Air fry at 350°F (175°C) for 10-12 minutes.

Notes

- Ensure that the carrot cake bites are spaced evenly in the air fryer basket to allow for proper air circulation, resulting in a uniformly cooked and delicious treat.

Nutritional Facts

Per Serving: **Kcal:** 150 **Fat:** 8 g **Carbs:** 20 g **Protein:** 3 g **Sugar:** 10 g

Cinnamon Vanilla Air Fried Pears

Cinnamon Vanilla Air Fried Pears

2 servings

5 min

12 min

Ingredients

- 2 ripe pears, halved and cored
- 1 tablespoon melted coconut oil
- 1 teaspoon vanilla extract
- 1/2 teaspoon ground cinnamon

Instructions

1. Preheat the air fryer to 360°F (180°C).
2. Brush pear halves with melted coconut oil and vanilla extract.
3. Sprinkle ground cinnamon on top.
4. Air fry for 10-12 minutes until pears are tender.

Notes

- The suggested cooking time may vary depending on the model and size of the air fryer, so monitor the pears closely to achieve the desired level of caramelization.

Nutritional Facts

Per Serving: **Kcal:** 160 **Fat:** 5 g **Carbs:** 35 g **Protein:** 5 g **Sugar:** 20 g

Walnut Banana Bread Bites

Walnut Banana Bread Bites

2 servings

5 min

12 min

Ingredients

- 2 ripe bananas, mashed
- 1/2 cup (60g) chopped walnuts
- 1/4 cup (30g) coconut flour
- 1 teaspoon cinnamon
- 1 tablespoon honey

Instructions

1. In a bowl, combine mashed bananas, chopped walnuts, coconut flour, cinnamon, and honey.
2. Form small bites and place them in the air fryer basket.
3. Air fry at 350°F (175°C) for 10-12 minutes.

Notes

- Keep a close eye on the bites as they cook. Cooking times can vary depending on the air fryer model. Begin checking for doneness at around 8 minutes, and adjust the cooking time accordingly to prevent over-browning.
- Feel free to customize the recipe by adding extra ingredients like shredded coconut, or raisins to suit your taste preferences.

Nutritional Facts

Per Serving: **Kcal:** 160 **Fat:** 8 g **Carbs:** 20 g **Protein:** 3 g **Sugar:** 10 g

Air Fryer Rosemary Peaches

Air Fryer Rosemary Peaches

2 servings

5 min

10 min

Ingredients

- 2 ripe peaches, halved and pitted
- 1 tablespoon melted coconut oil
- 1 tablespoon honey
- 1 teaspoon chopped fresh rosemary

Instructions

1. Preheat the air fryer to 360°F (180°C).
2. Brush peach halves with melted coconut oil and honey.
3. Sprinkle chopped rosemary on top.
4. Air fry for 8-10 minutes until peaches are tender and slightly caramelized.

Notes

- Use ripe yet firm peaches to withstand the cooking process.
- Be sure to preheat your air fryer to 360°F (180°C) before placing the peaches in the basket. The preheating process ensures even cooking and caramelization.

Nutritional Facts

Per Serving: **Kcal:** 120 **Fat:** 2.5 g **Carbs:** 30 g **Protein:** 1 g **Sugar:** 25g

Dessert Recipe Notes

Appendix A

Measurements and Variations

Essential Measurements: Precision in Every Bite

Unlock the full potential of your anti-inflammatory air frying journey with a solid understanding of essential measurements. This guide ensures accuracy in crafting your nutrient-rich, inflammation-fighting recipes. From liquids to dry ingredients, master the art of precise measuring.

Volume Measurements:

- 1 cup = 240 ml
- 1 tablespoon = 15 ml
- 1 teaspoon = 5 ml

Weight Measurements:

- 1 ounce = 28 grams
- 1 pound = 454 grams

Common Conversions:

- 1 cup quinoa = 185 grams
- 1 cup chopped vegetables = 150 grams
- 1 cup beans = 240 grams

Adapting Recipes: Tailoring for Wellness

In the realm of anti-inflammatory cooking, customization is key. This section empowers you to make recipes uniquely suited to your taste and dietary preferences. From ingredient substitutions to flavor enhancements, let your creativity shine.

Ingredient Substitutions:

- Replace refined oils with anti-inflammatory options like olive or avocado oil.
- Swap refined sugars with natural sweeteners like honey or maple syrup.
- Experiment with gluten-free flours for a grain-free alternative.

Customizing Flavors:

- Incorporate anti-inflammatory spices like turmeric, ginger, and cinnamon.
- Use fresh herbs such as basil, parsley, or cilantro for added flavor.
- Adjust salt levels and experiment with alternative seasonings.

Appendix B

Choosing the Perfect Air Fryer

Congratulations on your journey through the "Anti-Inflammatory Air Fryer Cookbook." Before you embark on your culinary adventure, let's delve into the world of air fryers and explore how to select the perfect one for your kitchen. Understanding the various types and features will empower you to make an informed decision, ensuring your cooking experience is seamless and enjoyable.

Understanding Different Types of Air Fryers:

Basket-Style Air Fryers:

- Ideal for individuals and small families.
- Efficient for cooking crispy and evenly browned dishes.

Oven-Style Air Fryers:

- Larger capacity, suitable for bigger families or gatherings.
- Often equipped with additional cooking functions beyond air frying.

Toaster Oven Air Fryers:

- Combines the functions of a toaster oven and air fryer.
- Great for those with limited kitchen space.

Convection Oven Air Fryers:

- Larger capacity with a powerful convection fan for quick and even cooking.
- Versatile, capable of handling various cooking styles.

Appendix C

WEEK 1 MEAL PLAN

	BREAKFAST	LUNCH	DINNER	SNACK
MON	Quinoa and Veggie Breakfast Bowl	Grilled Lemon Herb Chicken	Grilled Salmon with Sweet Potato Wedges	Sweet Potato Chips
TUE	Sweet Potato and Chickpea Hash	Quinoa and Roasted Vegetable Salad	Mediterranean Chicken Skewers	Kale Chips
WED	Salmon and Avocado Toast	Salmon with Dill Sauce	Turmeric Chicken Thighs with Roasted Vegetables	Garlic Parmesan Zucchini Chips
THUR	Spinach and Feta Stuffed Mushrooms	Sweet Potato Fries with Avocado Dip	Spinach and Feta Stuffed Turkey Burgers	Coconut Curry Chickpea Poppers
FRI	Blueberry Oat Muffins	Mediterranean Stuffed Bell Peppers	Balsamic Glazed Brussels Sprouts and Chicken	Sweet Potato Chips
SAT	Turkey and Vegetable Egg Cups	Turmeric-Ginger Salmon Patties	Eggplant Parmesan with Tomato Sauce	Cinnamon Apple Chips
SUN	Veggie Omelette with Smoked Salmon	Spinach and Mushroom Stuffed Chicken Breast	Spicy Chickpea & Vegetable Stir-Fry	Sweet and Spicy Roasted Nuts

WEEK 2 MEAL PLAN

	BREAKFAST	LUNCH	DINNER	SNACK
MON	Almond Flour Banana Pancakes	Cauliflower and Chickpea Shawarma Bowl	Lemon Garlicky Turkey Cutlets with Asparagus	Air Fried Salmon Bites
TUE	Avocado and Tomato Breakfast Quesadillas	Teriyaki Turkey Meatballs	Air Fryer Cauliflower & Chickpea Curry	Garlic Parmesan Zucchini Chips
WED	Brussels Sprouts and Bacon Frittata	Lemon Garlic Shrimp Skewers	Greek-style Turkey Burgers with Tzatziki	Crispy Brussels Sprouts
THUR	Almond Butter and Banana Stuffed French Toast	Zucchini Noodles with Pesto	Tofu Vegetable Stir-Fry	Sweet Potato Chips
FRI	Eggs and Spinach Breakfast Burrito	Greek Chicken Souvlaki Skewers	Air Fried Cilantro Lime Shrimp with Avocado Salsa	Cinnamon Apple Chips
SAT	Eggplant and Tomato Breakfast Stacks	Cumin-Spiced Roasted Carrot Salad	Pesto Chicken with Roasted Veggies	Kale Chips
SUN	Mediterranean Egg White Frittata	Caprese Stuffed Portobello Mushrooms	Butternut Squash and Chickpea Buddha Bowl	Coconut Crusted Shrimp

WEEK 3 MEAL PLAN

	BREAKFAST	LUNCH	DINNER	SNACK
MON	Apple Cinnamon Oatmeal Muffins	Spicy Cauliflower Bites	Caprese Stuffed Chicken Breasts	Garlic Parmesan Zucchini Chips
TUE	Cauliflower and Spinach Breakfast Hash Browns	Mediterranean Stuffed Sweet Potatoes	Moroccan Style Spiced Chicken Thighs with Cauliflower Rice	Sesame Ginger Edamame
WED	Peanut Butter Banana Wraps	Garlic Parmesan Asparagus Spears	Lemon Herb Cod with Roasted Broccoli	Air Fried Salmon Bites
THUR	Turmeric and Coconut Breakfast Quinoa	Lemon Herb Salmon Packets	Spaghetti Squash with Pesto Grilled Shrimp	Turmeric Roasted Chickpeas
FRI	Quinoa and Veggie Breakfast Bowl	Grilled Lemon Herb Chicken	Grilled Salmon with Sweet Potato Wedges	Coconut Crusted Shrimp
SAT	Sweet Potato and Chickpea Hash	Quinoa and Roasted Vegetable Salad	Mediterranean Chicken Skewers	Coconut Curry Chickpea Poppers
SUN	Salmon and Avocado Toast	Salmon with Dill Sauce	Turmeric Chicken Thighs with Roasted Vegetables	Crispy Brussels Sprouts

WEEK 4 MEAL PLAN

	BREAKFAST	LUNCH	DINNER	SNACK
MON	Spinach and Feta Stuffed Mushrooms	Sweet Potato Fries with Avocado Dip	Spinach and Feta Stuffed Turkey Burgers	Air Fried Salmon Bites
TUE	Blueberry Oat Muffins	Mediterranean Stuffed Bell Peppers	Balsamic Glazed Brussels Sprouts and Chicken	Garlic Parmesan Zucchini Chips
WED	Turkey and Vegetable Egg Cups	Turmeric-Ginger Salmon Patties	Eggplant Parmesan with Tomato Sauce	Turmeric Roasted Chickpeas
THUR	Veggie Omelette with Smoked Salmon	Spinach and Mushroom Stuffed Chicken Breast	Spicy Chickpea & Vegetable Stir-Fry	Sesame Ginger Edamame
FRI	Almond Flour Banana Pancakes	Cauliflower and Chickpea Shawarma Bowl	Lemon Garlicky Turkey Cutlets with Asparagus	Cinnamon Apple Chips
SAT	Avocado and Tomato Breakfast Quesadillas	Teriyaki Turkey Meatballs	Air Fryer Cauliflower & Chickpea Curry	Crispy Brussels Sprouts
SUN	Brussels Sprouts and Bacon Frittata	Lemon Garlic Shrimp Skewers	Greek-style Turkey Burgers with Tzatziki	Kale Chips

INDEX

A

B

C

S

T

V

W

Z

Made in United States
Cleveland, OH
30 November 2024

10912954R00101